18.95

MAR 3 2005

✓

7Y 8/09
10X 6/13
11Y 3/16
12X 12/17

Franklin D. Roosevelt

History Maker Bios

Laura Hamilton Waxman

LERNER PUBLICATIONS COMPANY • MINNEAPOLIS

*This book is inspired by and dedicated with love to my dad,
Dr. Bernard Waxman.*

Illustrations by Tim Parlin

Text and illustrations copyright © 2005 by Lerner Publications Company

Lerner Publications Company
A division of Lerner Publishing Group
241 First Avenue North
Minneapolis, MN 55401 U.S.A.

Website address: www.lernerbooks.com

Library of Congress Cataloging-in-Publication Data

Waxman, Laura Hamilton.
    Franklin D. Roosevelt / by Laura Hamilton Waxman.
        p.   cm. — (History maker bios)
    Includes bibliographical references and index.
    Contents: A perfect little gentleman—Franklin the leader—Challenging
times—"Nothing to fear"—"It must be done"—Timeline—A walk back in time.
    ISBN: 0-8225-1545-8 (lib. bdg. : alk. paper)
        1. Roosevelt, Franklin D. (Franklin Delano), 1882–1945—Juvenile literature.
2. Presidents—United States—Biography—Juvenile literature. [1. Roosevelt,
Franklin D. (Franklin Delano), 1882–1945. 2. Presidents.] I. Title. II. Series.
E807.W38 2005
973.917'092—dc22   2003026940

Manufactured in the United States of America
1 2 3 4 5 6 – JR – 10 09 08 07 06 05

TABLE OF CONTENTS

INTRODUCTION 5

1. A PERFECT LITTLE GENTLEMAN 6

2. FRANKLIN THE LEADER 13

3. CHALLENGING TIMES 19

4. "NOTHING TO FEAR" 27

5. "IT MUST BE DONE" 36

TIMELINE 44

A WALK BACK IN TIME 45

FURTHER READING 46

WEBSITES 46

SELECT BIBLIOGRAPHY 47

INDEX 48

FREEDOM UNDER THE STARS
WITH
JUSTICE AND SECURITY
FOR
ALL MANKIND

FRANKLIN D. ROOSEVELT

INTRODUCTION

Franklin D. Roosevelt was president of the United States longer than any other president in history. He was president during a difficult time known as the Great Depression. He also led the country through most of World War II.

As a leader, Franklin knew how to listen to people and earn their trust. He gave them hope when times were hard. He inspired millions of Americans to believe in their president, their nation, and themselves.

This is his story.

1 A PERFECT LITTLE GENTLEMAN

F ranklin Delano Roosevelt was born on January 30, 1882, in a beautiful mansion in Hyde Park, New York. His mother and father were the wealthy James and Sara Delano Roosevelt. They poured all their love and pride into their son. They taught him that he could do anything he set his mind to.

Franklin's childhood was filled with servants, long vacations in Europe, and sailing trips. Instead of going to school, he studied with private tutors. Instead of playing with other children, he spent most of his time alone or with adults. He worked on his stamp collection. He read book after book about sailing and the navy. And he learned how to be a perfect little gentleman.

A Funny Wish

When Franklin was seven years old, he met President Grover Cleveland. At the time, President Cleveland was struggling to win the next presidential election. He put his hand on young Franklin and said, "My little man, I am making a strange wish for you. It is that you may never be president of the United States." Luckily for Franklin, Cleveland's wish never came true!

When Franklin was fourteen years old, his parents enrolled him in Groton boarding school in Massachusetts. Some of the country's wealthiest families sent their sons to this school.

Franklin felt lonely at Groton. He didn't fit in with other boys his age. He had to learn how to get along with them—and it wasn't easy. Some of the boys disliked Franklin. He wasn't very good at sports. And he tried too hard to please others.

Franklin (CIRCLED) was on Groton's football team, but he was too lightweight to be a good player.

The school's principal was the Reverend Endicott Peabody. Reverend Peabody knew that most of his students planned to become bankers, lawyers, or businessmen. But he had other ideas. He encouraged his students to become politicians and help run the government.

Franklin knew something about politics. His fifth cousin, Theodore Roosevelt, was the governor of New York. Franklin admired Cousin Teddy's sharp mind and boundless energy. Teddy made being a politician seem exciting and rewarding.

Franklin admired his cousin Theodore Roosevelt (RIGHT).

Franklin (CENTER FRONT) worked on the HARVARD CRIMSON newspaper while he was a student at Harvard University.

Franklin graduated from Groton in 1900. He entered Harvard University that fall. This time, he was determined to win over his classmates. He was charming and confident. He made friends more easily and even became president of the school newspaper.

Theodore Roosevelt continued to fascinate Franklin. That November, Cousin Teddy was elected vice president of the United States. He would work alongside President William McKinley. Franklin kept up with all the latest news about his famous cousin.

At the same time, another Roosevelt caught Franklin's attention. Seventeen-year-old Eleanor Roosevelt was Teddy's favorite niece. Eleanor was shy, awkward, smart, and serious. But Franklin put her at ease with his usual charm. The two began to spend more and more time together.

Shy Eleanor saw a special spark in Franklin.

On March 17, 1905, Franklin married Eleanor. Theodore Roosevelt was then president of the United States. He walked his niece down the aisle.

The young couple moved to New York. Franklin was studying there to become a lawyer. In May 1906, Eleanor gave birth to Anna, the first of six children.

In 1907, a highly respected law firm in New York City hired Franklin. He was on his way to becoming a successful lawyer.

But Franklin had another dream. He told some friends at the law firm that he wanted to follow in Cousin Teddy's footsteps. Someday, he said, he would be president of the United States.

2 FRANKLIN THE LEADER

By 1910, twenty-eight-year-old Franklin had a plan. He was going to begin his political career in the state of New York.

Franklin wanted to run for state senate. This elected group of citizens helped make laws for all of New York. Franklin had just one problem. No one thought he could get elected.

Two main groups, the Democrats and the Republicans, fought to run the government. Franklin was a Democrat. Most of the people in his part of the state voted for Republicans.

Franklin's mind was set on winning the election. If it could be done, he told himself, he would do it.

Franklin traveled from town to town meeting voter after voter. Sometimes he gave twenty speeches in one day. The speeches made him nervous. But he loved talking to individual voters. He had a knack for making them trust him.

Franklin learned how to give powerful speeches to help him get elected.

In November 1910, Franklin D. Roosevelt did what people said he could not do. He won the election and became a state senator. Franklin knew this was only the beginning. He would have to win many more elections if he wanted to be president.

In 1913, President Woodrow Wilson offered Franklin an exciting job. The president wanted him to come to Washington, D.C., to be assistant secretary of the navy.

WORLD WAR I

World War I began in Europe while Franklin was working for the Department of the Navy. Tensions and rivalries had been building up among European nations. By the end of 1914, Great Britain, France, and Russia were fighting a war against Germany and Austria-Hungary. In 1917, the United States joined the fight too. World War I ended in 1918 with the defeat of Germany and its partners.

As the assistant secretary of the navy, Roosevelt (RIGHT, HOLDING HAT) inspects a navy ship in the New York Harbor. Eleanor (FAR LEFT) watches him.

The offer thrilled Franklin. He loved the idea of helping to run the U.S. Navy. Cousin Teddy had held the exact same job years earlier. Franklin happily accepted the offer. He spent seven years in Washington.

Other Democrats noticed Franklin's strengths as a leader. In 1920, they asked him to run for vice president. They had chosen the governor of Ohio, James M. Cox, as their candidate for president. Franklin knew that Cox had only a small chance of winning the election. But he agreed to run for vice president anyway.

Eleanor (BACK ROW, CENTER) lines up John, Franklin Jr., Elliot, Anna, and their dog Chief for a photo in 1920.

Franklin enjoyed the chance to get out and meet voters. Trains took him across the United States. Franklin gave speeches and met with voters. He saw how his fellow Americans lived. He listened to their hopes and dreams. He made people feel that their ideas mattered.

James M. Cox and Franklin Roosevelt lost the election. But Franklin had gained something important. He had begun to understand the people of his nation. He sensed what they wanted in a leader. And he was determined to become that kind of leader. If it could be done, he promised himself, he would do it.

A Cox-Roosevelt campaign poster

3 CHALLENGING TIMES

In 1921, Franklin took a break from politics. That summer, he joined his family for a holiday. He swam and sailed. He spent time with Eleanor and the children. Then he came down with a horrible illness.

At first, he simply felt tired and weak. But after several days, he could not move his legs. He learned that he had a disease called polio.

Many polio patients became paralyzed from the waist down. They ended up using wheelchairs or crutches.

Franklin put on a brave face for his family and friends. But inside, he was terrified. He wondered if he would ever walk again.

Franklin did everything he could do to make his legs move again. He tried different cures and doctors. He went to a health resort in Warm Springs, Georgia. He spent years trying to get better. But nothing worked.

WARM SPRINGS

The Warm Springs health resort in Georgia had pools of naturally warm mineral water. Some people believed the water could help cure polio patients. The resort was run-down when Franklin went there for the first time. He spent thousands of dollars fixing it up for other polio patients. Over the years, he made regular trips to Warm Springs to strengthen his legs and relax.

Franklin found ways to enjoy himself. Here he spends time fishing.

In the 1920s, most people expected someone with a disability to spend the rest of his or her life hidden away at home. No one would blame Franklin Roosevelt if he never ran for another election. After all, they thought, who would elect a man in a wheelchair? But Franklin was determined to live a normal life. It could be done, he told himself. And he *must* do it.

Franklin didn't want people to judge him unfairly for his disability. He practiced standing without crutches. He learned to lean on a cane with one hand. With the other hand, he held on tightly to his son or a friend. Franklin wore braces on his legs to help keep him steady. The braces went under his pants so people wouldn't notice them.

Franklin could stand and give speeches like any other politician. He even taught himself to move without a wheelchair. He learned to move his legs with his strong upper body. That way, he looked as though he could walk.

Eleanor and a friend named Louis Howe believed in Franklin. They encouraged him to return to politics. In 1928, Franklin ran for governor of New York.

All of Franklin's practice paid off. Voters hardly noticed the strange way he walked or all the times he sat instead of stood. They saw a man with a confident smile. They heard his powerful voice. They chose Franklin to be their next governor. He was forty-six years old.

Governor Roosevelt works at his desk in Albany, New York, the state capital.

Life changed for many people in the United States while Franklin was governor. A difficult time known as the Great Depression began in 1929. During the Great Depression, millions of people lost their jobs, their homes, and their savings.

Without money to spend, people couldn't afford to buy new products or fresh food. Companies went out of business. Farmers lost their farms. Without money to save, people closed their bank accounts. Many banks shut down.

During the Great Depression, unemployed and homeless people lined up at places called soup kitchens for a free meal that was usually a bowl of soup.

Many families lived in poverty during the Great Depression. Franklin wanted to help them.

At first, Franklin agreed with President Herbert Hoover. Both men thought the Great Depression would end soon. People could take care of themselves until then.

In less than a year, Franklin began to change his mind. He read letter after letter from needy New Yorkers. They were begging their governor for help. He had to do something. "The situation is serious," he said in a speech to reporters, "and the time has come for us to face this unpleasant fact."

Franklin faced the problems of his state fearlessly. He found ways to house the homeless and give money to the poor. He also worked to keep people in their jobs and to create new jobs for workers who needed them. No other governor did more to tackle the Great Depression.

Soon people began to talk about Franklin D. Roosevelt for president. Herbert Hoover planned to run for reelection in 1932 as the Republican candidate. The Democrats chose Franklin. He was ready.

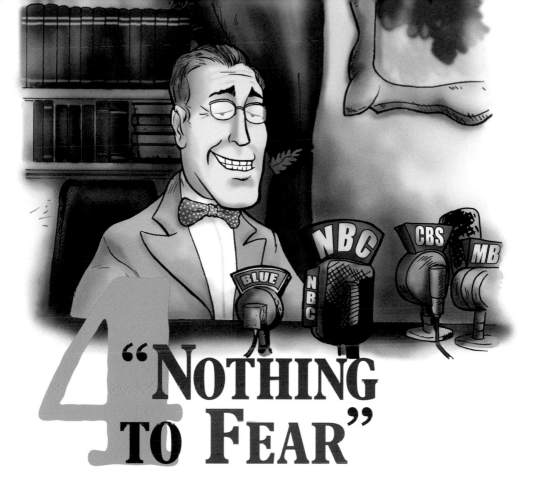

4 "NOTHING TO FEAR"

Franklin knew that many people felt hopeless and afraid. The Great Depression had only gotten worse. And no end was in sight. Franklin wanted to be a leader who could give people hope and take away their fears. Everywhere he went, he spoke confidently about the future. His smile and courage comforted voters.

Franklin promised that he would make people's lives better. He called his plan "a new deal for the American people." On election day in 1932, millions of voters chose Franklin Delano Roosevelt to be their next president.

Franklin gave his first speech as president on March 4, 1933. People all over the United States sat around their radios to listen. They heard their new president speak in a loud, clear voice.

Franklin and Eleanor smile confidently to the crowd when Franklin is sworn in as president.

RADIO DAYS

The radio was a new and exciting invention in the 1920s. By the time Franklin became president, radios were as common as televisions have become. People gathered around the radio to listen to the news and to follow their favorite radio programs. They also listened to speeches from their president. Franklin took full advantage of this new technology to reach millions of Americans.

He promised "to speak the truth, the whole truth, frankly and boldly." Then he declared, "The only thing we have to fear is fear itself." He asked the people of his country to come together and stand behind him and his ideas. With everyone's support, no problem was too big to solve.

Franklin's speech worked miracles. The mood of the country changed overnight. That week, thousands of letters flooded into the White House from grateful Americans. President Roosevelt had given them hope again. They trusted him.

Franklin knew he needed to keep earning their trust. He worked hard on his plan, the New Deal. The New Deal improved life for millions of people in the United States. It kept banks open. It helped farmers stay in business. And it gave work and money to millions of people without jobs.

A YOUNG MAN'S OPPORTUNITY

CCC

FOR WORK PLAY STUDY & HEALTH

APPLICATIONS TAKEN BY
ILLINOIS EMERGENCY RELIEF COMMISSION
ILLINOIS SELECTING AGENCY

Two important New Deal programs offered work. One program was called the Civilian Conservation Corps, or the CCC.

A CCC poster from Illinois offers jobs to young men.

This public sculpture was a WPA project built in California.

The CCC paid young men to keep the nation's forests, lakes, and parks in good condition. Corps workers learned new skills by planting trees, taking care of the land, and tending lakes and rivers.

The other program was the Works Progress Administration, or the WPA. The WPA paid men and women to construct or repair roads, bridges, and important buildings, such as schools and hospitals. It also provided work and money for artists, musicians, and writers.

Unemployed men sign up for help from the government.

In 1935, Franklin signed a law to give more help to people without jobs. The law was called the Social Security Act. The Social Security program collected taxes from businesses and workers. This money would be set aside and given to people after they retired. Several years later, the program also began helping children, people without jobs, and the disabled.

Not everyone liked President Roosevelt's New Deal. In fact, some people hated it—and hated Franklin for creating it. Wealthy citizens and business owners thought the president was spending too many of their tax dollars on the New Deal. And they believed he didn't have much to show for it. After all, the Great Depression was still a big problem.

But many more people still liked Franklin. They called him FDR. They thought of him as their friend and hero. Portraits of the president hung in homes, schools, bus stops, and barbershops.

Franklin worked hard to stay connected to the American people. Each week, he gave short, simple talks over the radio. Some of his more important speeches were called "fireside chats."

Franklin's popularity inspired people to display his portrait in their businesses and homes.

Franklin also held press conferences almost every day. During these conferences, reporters squeezed into his White House office. Franklin answered their questions. He also charmed the reporters with his bright smile and clever jokes. Never before had a president put himself in the spotlight the way Franklin did.

Eleanor Roosevelt also spent a lot of time in the spotlight. Most First Ladies stayed away from politics. Not Eleanor. People said she had become Franklin's legs.

Eleanor (CENTER) visits a WPA nursery school in Iowa.

She traveled all over the United States to check on Franklin's New Deal programs. She cared deeply for the people she saw. She wanted to make life better for them.

Each time that Eleanor came back from her travels, she shared her ideas with Franklin. She also shared her thoughts with the people of the United States. Six days a week, she wrote a newspaper column called "My Day." She changed the way people thought about the First Lady.

In the 1936 election, Franklin easily won another four-year term as president. During this second term, he continued to work hard to end the Great Depression. Franklin was not afraid to take risks to solve a problem. Sometimes he made mistakes. But he never lost hope. He wouldn't let the American people lose hope, either.

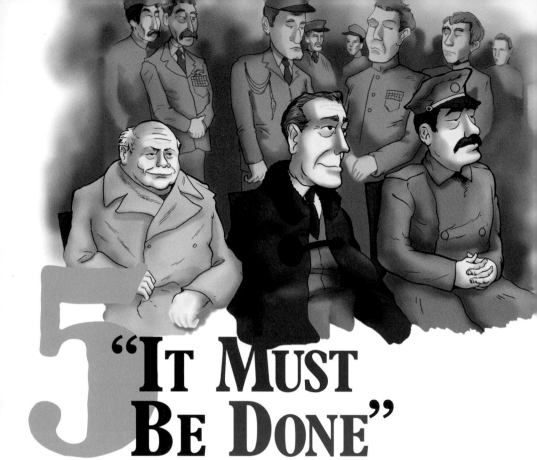

5 "IT MUST BE DONE"

In 1940, Franklin did something no other U.S. president had done before. He ran for a third term. Some people thought he had been president for too long. They wanted to give someone else a turn. But many more voters were happy with FDR. He won his third election for president in November 1940.

Franklin still worried about the Great Depression. But he also had something else to worry about. World War II had been going on in parts of Europe and Asia for more than a year. So far, the United States had stayed out of the war. But Franklin believed Americans would have to join the fight sooner or later.

Then, on December 7, 1941, Japan attacked the U.S. Navy in Pearl Harbor, Oahu, Hawaii. More than two thousand U.S. citizens died. Franklin called it "a date which will live in infamy." He knew the terrible attack would never be forgotten.

Bombs from Japanese planes started many fires in Pearl Harbor. The attack shocked U.S. citizens.

After that, the United States entered World War II. The country joined Great Britain, Russia, and many other countries to fight against Japan, Germany, and Italy.

Somehow, Franklin had to convince factories to help the United States win the war. He needed them to make thousands of weapons, tanks, planes, and ships in a short time. People told Franklin that his idea to build so many weapons so quickly was impossible. They said it couldn't be done. But Franklin knew better.

"Let no man say it cannot be done," he boomed in a speech to the U.S. Congress. "It must be done—and we have undertaken to do it."

Franklin asked everyone to take factory jobs.

Some schoolchildren during World War II made model airplanes for the U.S. military. The military used the models to train soldiers.

Franklin's words of hope and confidence inspired the country to support him. Workers in car, clothing, and even toy factories learned how to make war supplies. The factory owners needed many workers to run their new machines. People without jobs could work again. The Great Depression ended for good.

Franklin (CENTER) talks with Russian leader Joseph Stalin (LEFT) and British prime minister Winston Churchill (RIGHT) at a meeting in Tehran, Iran, in 1943.

During World War II, Franklin met with the leaders of Russia and Great Britain to discuss the best way to win the war. By the summer of 1944, Franklin saw that victory was near. He had a difficult choice to make. He had finished his third term as president. Should he run again?

Franklin was tired. He had been president for nearly twelve years. He was sixty-two years old and had many health problems. He dreamed of returning to his childhood home in Hyde Park.

But Franklin also had big plans for his country's future. He didn't want those plans ignored. He ran for president again and won.

World peace was on Franklin's mind. World War II had destroyed cities and cost millions of lives. Franklin wanted to unite the countries of the world in peace. He dreamed of an organization called the United Nations.

Franklin did not live to see the United Nations take shape. He died in Warm Springs, Georgia, on April 12, 1945. World War II ended less than five months later.

THE UNITED NATIONS

The United Nations officially formed on October 24, 1945. It began with fifty-one countries. But it has grown to include almost two hundred nations. True to Franklin's dream, the United Nations is dedicated to preventing war. It also protects the rights of people everywhere to live freely and to be treated with dignity.

Franklin's death saddened millions of people. After he died, a train brought him back to Washington, D.C., for a presidential funeral. Along the way, people lined the railroad tracks for miles. Some people cried or waved handkerchiefs as the train went by. Others stood quietly in memory of their friend and hero.

Horses pull Franklin's flag-draped coffin (FAR RIGHT) along the streets of Washington, D.C.

Franklin gave hope and courage to the nation.

Franklin D. Roosevelt inspired Americans to believe in themselves and their president. He showed them that nothing was impossible. By his own example, he taught them that the only thing they had to fear was fear itself.

TIMELINE

FRANKLIN DELANO ROOSEVELT WAS BORN ON JANUARY 30, 1882.

In the year . . .

1896 Franklin enrolled in Groton boarding school. `Age 14`

1900 he entered Harvard University.

1903 he graduated from Harvard with a degree in history.

1904 he studied law at Columbia University.

1905 he married Eleanor Roosevelt on March 17. `Age 23`

1907 he got a job at a law firm in New York.

1910 he was elected to the New York State Senate.

1913 President Woodrow Wilson appointed him assistant secretary of the navy.

1920 Franklin ran for vice president of the United States. `Age 38`

1921 he became ill with polio.

1928 he was elected governor of New York.

1929 the Great Depression began in the United States. `Age 50`

1932 he was elected the thirty-second president of the United States.

1936 he won his second term as president.

1940 he became the only president to win a third term.

1941 Japan attacked Pearl Harbor, Hawaii, on December 7.
the United States entered World War II.

1944 he won a fourth term as president. `Age 63`

1945 he died on April 12.

A WALK BACK IN TIME

Imagine that you could go back in history to the time when Franklin was president. Visitors to the Franklin Delano Roosevelt Memorial in Washington, D.C., do just that.

This large national monument includes an outdoor room for each of Franklin's four presidential terms. Inside the rooms, life-sized sculptures show Franklin as president. And some of his famous words are displayed on the walls.

The memorial also includes sculptures of everyday Americans and events in history. One sculpture is of a man listening to a "fireside chat" on the radio. Another shows people struggling to survive the Great Depression.

In the park's main area is a timeline. It lists the important dates and events in Franklin's amazing life.

A sculpture in the Franklin Delano Roosevelt Memorial shows Franklin sitting by one of his favorite dogs, Fala.

FURTHER READING

NONFICTION
Isaacs, Sally Senzell. *America in the Time of Franklin Delano Roosevelt: 1929 to 1948.* **Chicago: Heinemann Library, 2000.** Explores life in the United States while FDR was alive.

Swain, Gwenyth. *Theodore Roosevelt.* **Minneapolis: Lerner Publications Company, 2005.** A biography of Franklin's famous relative, the twenty-sixth president of the United States.

Whitman, Sylvia. *Children of the World War II Home Front.* **Minneapolis: Carolrhoda Books, Inc., 2001.** Explores the lives and experiences of children and their families in the United States during World War II.

Winget, Mary. *Eleanor Roosevelt.* **Minneapolis: Lerner Publications Company, 2003.** A biography of the life and work of Eleanor Roosevelt.

FICTION
Winthrop, Elizabeth. *Franklin Delano Roosevelt: Letters from a Mill Town Girl.* **Delray Beach, FL: Winslow Press, 2001.** Twelve-year-old Emma Bartoletti corresponds with her president, Franklin D. Roosevelt, about how the Great Depression has affected her and her family.

WEBSITES

America's Library
<http://www.americaslibrary.gov> Find out more about the people and history of the United States through games, movies, and songs. Click on "Jump Back in Time" to learn more about the Great Depression and World War II.

Franklin D. Roosevelt Presidential Library and Museum
<http://www.fdrlibrary.marist.edu/educat33.html> Browse historical documents and photos, and complete on-line activities to learn more about Franklin and Eleanor Roosevelt.

United Nations Cyberschoolbus
<http://www.un.org/Pubs/CyberSchoolBus/index.asp> Learn about the role of the United Nations and what you can do to improve the lives of people all over the world.

SELECT BIBLIOGRAPHY

Davis, Kenneth S. *FDR: The Beckoning of Destiny, 1882–1928.* New York: G. P. Putnam's Sons, 1972.

Davis, Kenneth S. *FDR: Into the Storm, 1937–1940.* New York: Random House, 1993.

Davis, Kenneth S. *FDR: The New York Years, 1928–1933.* New York. Random House, 1985.

Davis, Kenneth S. *FDR: The War President, 1940–1943.* New York: Random House, 2000.

Morgan, Ted. *FDR: A Biography.* New York: Simon & Schuster, 1985.

Roosevelt, Franklin Delano. *The Presidential Papers of Franklin Delano Roosevelt.* CD-ROM. Lindon, UT: CDex Information Group, 1995.

Ward, Geoffrey C. *Before the Trumpet: Young Franklin Roosevelt, 1882–1905.* New York: Harper & Row, 1985.

Ward, Geoffrey C. *A First-Class Temperament: The Emergence of Franklin Roosevelt.* New York: Harper & Row, 1989.

INDEX

childhood, 6–9
children, 12, 17, 19, 22
Cleveland, Grover, 7
Cox, James M., 17, 18

fireside chats, 33, 45
Franklin Delano Roosevelt
    Memorial, 45

Germany, 15, 38
Great Britain, 15, 38, 40
Great Depression, 5, 24–27, 35,
    37, 39, 45
Groton Boarding School, 8–9

Harvard University, 10
hobbies, 7, 8, 10, 21
Hoover, Herbert, 25, 26
Hyde Park, 6, 40

Japan, 37, 38

McKinley, William, 10

navy, 7, 15–16, 37
New Deal, 28–32, 35
New York State, 6, 12, 13,

23, 25; state senator for,
    13–15; governor of, 23–26
Pearl Harbor, 9
pets, 17, 45
polio, 19–22
president of the United States,
    5, 7, 12, 15, 26, 28–43, 45

radio, 29, 33, 45
Roosevelt, Eleanor, 11–12, 16,
    17, 19, 22, 23, 28, 34–35
Roosevelt, Theodore (Teddy),
    9, 10, 12, 16
Russia, 15, 38, 40

Social Security Program, 32
speeches, 14, 18, 22, 28–30, 38

United Nations, 41

Warm Springs, Georgia, 20, 42
Washington, D.C., 15–16, 42,
    45
Wilson, Woodrow, 15
work programs, 26, 30–32
World War I, 15
World War II, 5, 37–42

Acknowledgments

For photographs and artwork: Library of Congress, pp. 4 (LC-USZ62-120408), 9 (LC-USZ62-7220), 25 (LC-USF-000553-M4), 30 (LC-USZC2-862), 42 (LC-USZ62-67439), 43 (LC-USZ62-117439); Franklin D. Roosevelt Library, pp. 8, 10, 11, 14, 17, 18, 21, 22, 23, 28, 32, 34, 38, 40; Army War College, courtesy of the Franklin D. Roosevelt Library, p. 16; National Archives, pp. 24, 31 (NWDNS-RG-69-N-23478), 39 (NWDNS-208-NP-3KK-1); © The Brett Weston Archive/CORBIS, p. 33; © Three Lions/SuperStock, p. 37; © Richard T. Nowitz/CORBIS, p. 45.
Front cover: Franklin D. Roosevelt Library.
Back cover: © Todd Strand/Independent Picture Service.